Wizard

Dominic Berry

Flapjack Press
www.flapjackpress.co.uk

First published in 2011 by Flapjack Press
Chiffon Way, Trinity Riverside, Gtr Manchester
www.flapjackpress.co.uk

ISBN-13: 978 0 9570141 1 4

Cover design by Brink & Dominic Berry, 2011
Author photographs by ianwallisphotography.co.uk

Illustrated by Brink, 2011
www.paulneads.co.uk

Printed & bound in Great Britain by Direct-POD
Saxon Fields, Brixworth, Northampton
www.direct-pod.com

Wizard

Following a full capacity debut at Contact Theatre, Manchester Literature Festival and Nuyorican Poetry Café slam champion Dominic Berry returns as Wizard, one man struggling to fit in. In a unique world born of *Dungeons & Dragons,* Japanese RPGs and Greek myths, this heartfelt, honest collection mixes a poetry-spouting kettle, hilarious spell-casting dish rack and the true horror of a broken mental health system.

A Manchester-based artist, Dominic co-hosted greenroom's *Freed Up* open mic for five years. He continues to coordinate a multitude of events and workshops across the northwest. In 2010 his Arts Council funded *West Verse East* project saw him explore new writing with Buddhist and jazz influences. In January 2012 he made his directing debut with The Lowry's poetry play, *Working Verse presents Amateur Thematics.*

"I was taken by his energy, charm and, poetic prowess. Dominic is a committed and passionate artist who not only shines individually but is an advocate for other poets. As an individual Dominic's poetry is at once poignant, personal, profound, and humorous. He is a talented performer who brings a dynamic physicality and theatricality to the realm of poetry."
Baba Israel, Artistic Director, Contact

By the same author:

poetry
Tomorrow, I Will Go Dancing

adventure gamebook
Lyric of Dragon Claw Keep

Dedicated to Grandma,
thank you for always believing in me, always supporting
me and always being there with lots of love. I'm the luckiest
grandson to ever don a wizard's hat.
I love you loads.
xxx

Acknowledgements

Earlier versions of 'Stranger Dress' and 'Sellotaped Smile' were printed in the *Foreword* anthology, published by Route.

'Do Ken and Ryu Cuddle After Fights' was first published online by *Poetry 24*.

'Suzanne Takes Me Down' was originally printed in the *Sub Verse* collection with greenroom.

Earlier versions of 'My Living Document', 'To Your Party' and 'Peace of Vegan Cake' were printed in *The Ugly Tree*, published by Flapjack Press.

'Princess' was originally printed in *The Best of Manchester Poets, Volume 2*, published by Puppywolf Press.

'Into the Sea', 'We Swim Together', 'Steve', 'Medusa', 'Sun', 'Hero', 'Earth', 'Snail' and '4am' were written and developed as part of Dominic's Arts Council England Grants for the Arts funded *West Verse East* project, as were the following poems that went on to feature in the *Wizard* script: 'Tea', 'The Elders' Song', 'Zombies', 'Gorgons', 'Imp or Giant', 'Shape-Shifter' and 'Strangers Talk'.

'Playing Mortal Kombat' was first published online in *www.mortalkombatonline.com*.

Contents

Stranger Dress

my first poem performed, Slam Bam Thank You Ma'am, *Christmas 1999*

One day, when I was bored,
I dressed myself in strangers.
They made me feel beautiful,
pushed diamonds in my lap.
And there were wild, flashing colours
everywhere my heart touched.

And every frown I saw became
a harbour to a smile.
And every sobbing drunk I touched
was sober... for a while.

Threw off all the rags I'd worn,
I'd been a slave to labels.
Never even realised
all this freedom could be mine!
So, pull out the panic
from me celebrating madness,

I know
my wardrobe doesn't have a thing to wear through rain.
I know
that all my jewels are fake as any artist sane.
I know
that all the men I wear, like cloth, will quickly fade,

but still I'm glad when I got bored
I chose the clothes that suit me!

Dolled up like a princess,
I won't go home today.
I grabbed a fist of fancy jewels
and never had to pay.

I'll never miss the drab, grey
tatters I wore yesterday,
'cos the first time you feel happy
can never be taken away.

I first encountered Dominic Berry in 1999 at *Slam Bam Thank You Ma'am,* an event run by the incredible Chloe Poems (Gerry Potter) in a smoky mezzanine at greenroom, Manchester. We were both nervous 'open mic' virgins. Dominic's delivery was vibrant and faster than a speeding bullet; he was and still is compulsive viewing.

Over the course of a few years we grew as performers, became proud winners of the 'Silver Stake' at Rosie Lugosi's *Creatures of The Night* and moved from 'open mic' slots to supporting guest spots to headlining and winning slams on the Manchester, regional and national poetry scenes.

We were both incredibly inspired by the way in which Gerry and Rosie created a totally accepting atmosphere and championed inclusivity by providing a space for people to express their identity – whatever that might be. We both feel we wouldn't be poets today without their energy, help and encouragement.

Sadly, through pressure of work I drifted away from the poetry scene for number of years. Upon my recent return I found Dominic Berry continuing to spread the ethos set by Gerry and Rosie. He has become a magnificent creative driving force behind the Manchester poetry scene hosting a plethora of events and workshops along the way including a five year stint leading *Freed Up* at Manchester's greenroom.

My first night back as an 'open mic' performer was like returning home after a long and difficult journey. There to welcome me at the door with open heart and mind was my darling Dominic bouncing around a stage as co-host at *Poets Get Mashed* – he is *still* an absolute tornado!

Within a few weeks I was working alongside Martin Stannage,

Rod Tame and Benny-Jo Zahl on Dominic's poetry play, *Wizard*. I bagged the part of Ursula, the ghost of a menopausal midwife who inhabits Wizard's kettle. Rehearsing the play gave me an incredible confidence boost and performing it at Manchester's Contact was an absolute ball.

Dominic's words transport me to places where I would never knowingly walk alone. His work reaches out and triggers the colours, scents and echoes of deeply disturbing moments faced by many, if not us all, at some time in our lives.

Mental illness is a social taboo. Those who suffer because of it are stigmatised in this society. Wizard never goes outside anymore. He weaves spells to protect against the overpowering interference of social services and people who just don't understand. The play reveals the loves, fears and panic of a person struggling to find ways to cope. To Wizard, the supermarket is an evil and terrifying place. His memories cage and torment him. So, he weaves a fantasy world and lives inside a mind where Ursula the poetry spouting kettle makes him smile and Daisuke the dish rack conquers all.

Wizard *is* magic. Dominic Berry *is* magic; a powerful poet and performer, an honest man and a beautiful champion of those whose voices are seldom heard.

I always listen to what he has to say.

Jo Warburton

Introduction

Thanks for buying / borrowing / finding / stealing this book. Thank you for reading poetry.

I love seeing people discover modern poetry and realising how massive its affect can be. But on a national scale, where mainstream entertainment has ever decreasing content (except *Doctor Who*) it seems our world isn't yet big enough to cope with something so intimate and raw. One day my poetry hero Gerry Potter will have his own primetime BBC1 show and his poem 'The Imagination Is God' (look it up on YouTube) will be Number 1 on a resurrected *Top of the Pops*. Until that day, 99% of this world has nothing to offer me.

That 1% left is the UK poetry scene. Not hip-hop, not music, not comedy - poetry. That 1% is everything to me. I don't like it when events try and merge poetry with other stuff. It's like trying to eat a mouth-watering meal of delicate tastes and fragrances right after being force-fed a mountain of fiery hot vindaloo. You're not in a great state to enjoy the subtleties and artistry of the skilled poet if some stand-up has been shouting rape jokes at you for half an hour.

Poetry events where the audience are allowed to focus on the writing and the sound of language are where I'm at my happiest. Some say mixing poetry and theatre, to perform poetry, dilutes true poetics. I say a page poet is someone who never ever speaks their poetry aloud. The second that work is spoken, it is performed poetry. It is theatre. I believe to be a good speaker of poetry you need theatre skills. That can perhaps be loud and flamboyant like my big, camp self, but it doesn't have to be. Hearing Leonard Cohen calmly recite 'A Thousand Kisses Deep' is theatre at its most electrifying (as is seeing Salford poet Kieren King performing his beautifully intense version of it, which I recently experienced during a spontaneous street gig one night when the venue we were meant to be in closed down without telling us). I have never seen a poem performed well read off an iPhone.

I'd hoped I'd find the sense of belonging I feel on the poetry scene across the gay scene. I didn't. I was bullied for being poor, bullied for being effeminate and bullied for not being drunk / stoned / pilled-up enough. Like school! And here was me thinking Canal Street would be a gathering of all the battered intellectuals, savaged by school, ready to come together in truth, friendship and caring. No. After the hell of secondary education it was the poetry scene that gave this.

I was never beaten up at school but the threat of it punctured every day. I was good at running. I would be chased by groups of boys who'd throw stones, bricks and glass at me. Many a break time I spent pressing my back against the inside of a toilet cubicle door while fists and boots pounded against the other side. Faceless voices called me 'gay' while the school staff who did see pretended they didn't. In those horrific days of Clause 28, teachers were told that if they even thought the word 'gay' they would turn their entire class into hyper-gay-nymphomaniacs, were-gays foaming at the lips, mutant gays with extra eyes, tentacles and unnatural passions for Kylie Minogue.

Poetry has given me friends, confidence, laughs and a chance to talk and listen. And dance! I was about 21, dancing in Fab Café with Gerry Potter one St Patrick's Day, when a group of drunk men came in and starting calling us queer. Gerry kept dancing and he told me I should keep dancing. We danced together while drunk men called us queer and I've never felt so strong.

The poets I like are ones who always try new things, always listen to their audience and work to improve. It upsets me when poets get arrogant and stop noticing or caring if audiences like them. We as poets are fighting against a popular belief that all poetry is long, boring and rubbish, and it is terrible to watch poets whose work is all of the above being given a guest set just because they're someone's mate. Giving big performance opportunities to poets that audiences don't enjoy damages the poetry scene.

Having said that, those events aren't the majority and there is not a day that goes by when I don't think how lucky I am, getting to go all over the shop sharing my poems and doing what I love.

I've spoken loads about performance and I want to develop my poetry even further into theatre. That's how many of my poems came to form the *Wizard* script in this book. I'm excited by the prospect of touring the show and getting these poems to a different crowd in a different way. But that is not to overlook how significant poetry on the page is to me.

I am so proud to be published by Flapjack alongside so many of my favourite writers - my label mates - Ben Mellor, Jackie Hagan, Rosie Garland and, of course, Mr Gerry Potter. The poetry books I carry around with me in my little 'Queen Is Dead' bag are my rescue remedies. They are safe places I can dive into on a bus or in a shopping centre or at the side of a busy street when I am away from the poetry scene and life sometimes feels a bit too cruel.

If, like me, you find 99% of your own existence quite difficult then these poems are definitely for you. If you look like someone off *Hollyoaks* or have a personalised number plate or enjoy playing golf with your own father, then perhaps these poems might not be for you. Or maybe they are for you; maybe they'll turn you green-skinned and vegan, dig up your deeply repressed passion for villanelles and send you dancing naked through the streets shouting quotes by Oscar Wilde.

I hope so.

Dominic X

P.S. If you have a job you hate, leave.

Into The Sea

for long, summer days on a small, pebble beach

Worries, earth off cliffs, crumbling to ocean.
Worries erode

then salt winds hook nostrils and tug.

Excited feet quicken across smooth pebbles and
slash
sharp waves.
Cupped hands break surface,
full breath, head under.

Gull screams smothered as ears flood fill,
eyes sting thrill,
thighs seaweed slap.
I dive.
Breath and body release beneath air, beneath time,
it is not Monday here,
Monday means nothing.

Beneath my normal life where I am anchored to the dry
I can swim without names,
full breath, head under.

We Swim Together

I walk here,
my bare skin hugged by hot summer air.

Sky's more relaxed here.
No jostling against tower blocks with no idea of personal space,
polluting mornings with their monstrously polite words,
colossal resentments covered by appropriate work-wear.

Don't wear clothes here.

Naked feet pad from grass to pebble beach.
Naked eyes greet sea.

"Hiya, sea!"

A large, round face stares quizzically back.
A face that would suit a monocle.

It's a seal.

Never knew seals were so massive.
Never knew seals so suited monocles...

He watches, silent chuckling, as I inch my fumbly way
from blazing land into chilling water.
Never knew what the arched bits of my feet were for.
Underwater, iced toes clench
as sharp stones slice soft arches.
If I wore shoes less, my feet might be tougher.

I might be tougher.

Deeper. Deeper.
Take forever.
Seal still watching.
His quiet face communicates a hundred gentle words,
too gentle for voice,
letting me know what's what.
I am his guest and want to impress, but I know nothing
about sea.
Feel really naked.

Seal doesn't care.
We swim together
and I never knew not knowing mattered so little.

Swim together.
Take forever
together

and sea feels warmer than land.

My Living Document

4am parched, mine marches on paper legs.
Runs over its own mistakes again.
Parasitic bloated hungry,
mine is a vampire cannibal draining its own neck.
Stamping new ideas on top of old,
mine bleeds past thoughts between present ones,
jibes sour stories it promises tomorrow will unfold.
I've paper-cut eyes and fistfuls of scribble
that can't punch through even the lightest of doubts.
Gasping. Straining its leash.
This brittle cover can't hold mine down.
It tears ahead of hands, rips through pride and pants.
Its inky print stains you. My mouth says sorry.

Help me keep its wet, jaw pages tight shut.
A black blob butterfly waits inside, cackles all night.
How can I sleep? I am wide-eyed beside you.

Yours, in a dream-hammock over your head,
returns to your brain as you wake.
I wrestle with mine 'til it knocks me out cold.

Do Ken and Ryu Cuddle After Fights?

for all who play Street Fighter II

Do Ken and Ryu cuddle after fights?
They must need comfort after all they face.
Believing this might get me through my nights.

Such pumped testosterone surely invites
the kind of hug some men think a disgrace.
Do Ken and Ryu cuddle after fights?

Do lovely snuggles make them high as kites?
It's not just brawls, it's nuzzles these two chase!
Believing this might get me through my nights.

Can love and anger, both felt at their heights,
give something more than guilt as heartbeats race?
Do Ken and Ryu cuddle after fights?

In my mind's eye I see such tender sights.
Does Ryu spurt *"HA...DOU...KEN!"* mid-embrace?
Believing this might get me through my nights.

When I'm alone, my PlayStation invites
me to a violent, thrilling, frightful place.
Do Ken and Ryu cuddle after fights?
Believing this might get me through my nights.

Suzanne Takes Me Down

for Leonard Cohen's magical first song on his first LP

A stone-headed sailor capsized in sweaty duvet,
I am eleven, alone and ill.
Mouth, orange-peel dry;
eyes, torn flowers in garbage-heavy skull.
Want to swap my sick bits for better ones.

Wrap eyes in soothing lids, ears in radio and

> *Suzanne takes me down.*
> *My mind upon a river.*
> *Picture boats go by us,*
> *through every sweat-drenched shiver.*

This tune becomes a womb.
I'm regressing with the chord flow.
My foggy mind releases
this sick body to the undertow

> *for new, unbitten nails,*
> *a different length of finger,*
> *arms and waist, another flesh,*
> *with thighs and calves so slender.*

I want the opposite of me.
She holds the mirror still.
Suzanne's all rags and feathers.
Not eleven, alone or ill.

Seraphina

If you could go anywhere,
where would you go?
Do you know?
Where even in dimmest, grimmest night,
buried in the sky there is a... hidden glow.

This is a place
with a star-crossed patch of forever
that holds a henna-speckled magic
you will never struggle to uncover
whenever you need it,
because it's up there just for you.
Always.

This is a place dipped in song,
chocolate in glitter;
this is a place made out of chocolate cake, glitter,
laughter, henna and stars!

This is a country that's in Africa
and in Europe,
in Wonderland and Never-Never
where Peter Pan will teach your pony to fly,
and Alice
has told that cheeky Mad Hatter
to keep your days topped up with chuckle,
chatter
and dance!

I saw a Chuckle.
His name is George.

Sometimes George prrrrrrrrrrrrrs Hebrew lullabies.
Sometimes George meows naughty words!

George showed me this big, old sewing machine,
said I could sew a path to this place
from pink and scarlet wishes.
I did
and sailed there on a Fairy God Father's dream.

2 Fairy God Fellows,
1 Mum,
2 Dads
and 1 clowning brother
have juggled up this world all for you,
blessing your every step.

Nowhere else are clovers greener.
Click your heels, Seraphina.
Drooly George licks paw pads cleaner.
Click your heels, Seraphina.
Sugar clouds will rain Ribena!
Click your heels, Seraphina.
Blackcurrant sailing gondolier.
Click your heels, Seraphina.

Click your heels and sail
where love is as strong as a unicorn's horn
pointing toward your future steps.
Dancing forward.
Always dancing.
Always magic.
Seraphina.
Always loved.

Steve

Batman in a flat cap.
Poet in a pub.
Steve's tongue arches northern lights,
whips words like bat-a-rangs.
Cuts deep.
Stings.
Saves lives.

Recalls ancient lore.
Has out-stared demons I know
I couldn't face.

His sorcery encased pen nib
documents disaster, love
and café natter
with equal respect.
Suicide and chips.
Ennui and funk.

His poems outfunk Prince's 'Bat Dance'!

Raw romantic, he
purples blues with lune-lit truths,
illuminates sunset's clouds.

To Your Party

Take him to your party and the memories you've placed
before an almost endless line of men you once embraced.
You'll leave him with the evidence of all you have to waste.
These thieves who steal each other left him nameless in their haste.

Take him to your party and remind him all their names
and every burnt out promise from the ones you loved and blamed.
Then, maybe, from the embers of embarrassment and shame
he will, like you, find he forgets how quickly they all came.

He said, *"We all feel equal, all our visitors undressed."*
You used to feel ugly then you brushed him off your chest.
Take him to your party where the smiles so neatly rest.
However many times he leaves you
he knows he'll always be your guest.

Like Moonshine Pulls Moths

for Gary

Jam pots for egg cups. Ripped undies for cloths.
He's careful with money. He's frugal (*not* tight!).
Drawn to his studies like moonshine pulls moths.

Shabby chic meals. Makes banquets from broths.
No expense incurred! Delicious, despite
jam pots for egg cups, ripped undies for cloths.

Old books collect him like black clothes find goths.
Wrapped in their ancestry, read by starlight,
drawn to his studies like moonshine pulls moths.

Teaches kids history's passions and wraths.
"Learn from past errors. Recycle what's right."
Jam pots for egg cups, ripped undies for cloths.

Sure, some won't listen, sat sleepy as sloths,
but some feel his thought-sparking lessons excite,
drawn to his studies like moonshine pulls moths.

One wise man's voice can cut life-changing swaths
across open minds, set brain cells alight.
Jam pots for egg cups. Ripped undies for cloths.
Drawn to his studies like moonshine pulls moths.

Medusa

Ingrowing nails.
Sat behind the supermarket till,
chewing gnarled fingers.
Customers tut, *"Tsk! Tsk!"*
One day, stopped painting them.
Realised she'd got more nail in her than out.
An inside out pin cushion.
Spiky Medusa chewing.

One day, woke up with ingrowing hair.
Screaming, hissing migraines. Head full of cobras.
Felt like an atlas had cracked in her skull.
Felt like she'd swallowed the weather.
Got two months away from the shop
then Doctor said she was better.
Confided her eyes still twisted of serpents,
but Doctor said she was better.

He said she must smile.
Take the bandages offered for her internal bleeding.
Counterfeit concern.
The minimum rest keeps her stressed
python-knotted shoulders taut, chest crushed tight.

She wishes she could turn more than his heart to stone.

Lumps of fear, chunks of doubt
feed the snakes she can't carve out.

Sellotaped Smile

You sellotape a smile on.

You seal the holes excused as goals,
but residue seeps through.
As smiles peel,
feel tacky,
quickly, smack your face on any wall
to keep it all held firmly back.
You smack that smile flat and say,
"I'm smashing"
to fit in.

You sellotape a smile on,
but the bruise is glued within.

Princess

for a girl I saw one night, flyering for a nightclub, dressed as a Disney Princess

Not a real princess.
On the corner of Midnight and Spirit,
achingly sober, shaved armpits,
smiling a bent moonbeam,
paid to stand and wait.

You could have seen she was no princess
in the snow white of her eye
when he told her: *"You are a princess,"*
when he told her: *"Show some thigh.*
Flip that frown. Wake up, Beauty,
smell the coffee liqueur.
Half price booze! We are open 'til four.
Shout it loud! Make me proud.
Show some shoulder. Lose that bra.
Bring our lads in. Fill my bar."

But she didn't feel like a princess
on the corner of Midnight and Spilled Spirit Staining,
fumbling out flyers,
smiling,
smiling.
Felt like an origami swan made from unpaid bills,
paid to stand and wait.

This world will never want her skills.
She could make a Crystal Castle with just pasta and glue,
knew twelve ways to cheat at a Rubik's Cube,
could make up great voices for pencils,

but
she worked for a bar
in a strapless bra
on the corner of Midnight and Empty.

Then seven little men
got too close.
Boozy, Schmoozy, Handsy, Shouty,
Licky, Pukey and Punch
said hello,

"Hi... ho!"

"Nice legs. When do they open?"
"D'you like chicken? This cock'll have you chokin'."
"Don't put out your goods if you're not selling too."
"If you were my daughter, I would still be bathing you."

She knew she was no princess.
Loyal to her boss, her Prince Harming,
she'd faced these little men,
these mice disguised as stallions,
rodents wrapped in beer sticky manes.
"Neigh. Squeak! Neigh."

The customer isn't always bright

but she was.

Brighter than any crown,
that was the day
she walked away.

She walked away
and their taunts turned to fairy dust,
insults dissolved, shadows clouding into candy floss.
Walked away, body full of sunrise,
skin a goose bump farm.
Honk! Honk!
Cleared the road!
Ripped down the corner of Midnight.
Spirit of Kate Bush, Lionheart, twilight.
Wow - Wow - Wowed through morning,
Spirit to Swift Wind,
blizzards of light hope quivered her lungs
and Rubik's Cube squares flitted free her feet
like Billie Jean!

She walked away.

Now,
she might be inventing the rechargeable biro.
Might be baking the first daffodil pie.
She might have become a princess...
or anything.

The Colossal Monster of Cannot

Just because some people don't believe in monsters
doesn't mean they don't exist.

The Colossal Monster of Cannot loves being not believed in.
Means it doesn't have to hide under beds or inside wardrobes.
Doesn't have to fight.
Feasts.
It's growing,
invisible, invincible, gorging on worry,
smacking its belly over my eyes.

It tells me
a gay like me
will never play sports professionally,
at least, not safely.

The Monster crowns itself undisputed champ.
I'm dismissed as fairy-weight,
told I'm too out for the count.

If everyone believed The Monster was real
we might be able to stop it existing,

but this Monster knows its best attack
is making you feel too weak to fight back.

Julie Jones VS The Colossal Monster of Cannot

for Julie, who has fired-up so many to question and protest

Rrrrroll up! Rrrrroll up!
It's The Colossal Monster of Cannot VS... Julie Jones!
What a furore!
What a foe!
What a fight!

Here is The Colossal Monster of Cannot.
It loves seeing people pulverised with greed
and what TV says we need
in our hope of turning debt to diamond.
Loves hearing people celebrate inequality,
cheers us on.
"Hey!
Feast your eyes on everything
that you will never be."

Ding! Ding!

In the red corner:
it is Julie Jones!
Weighing in at... ... ...well, she'd rather not say,
a retired Uni lecturer from Manchester today.

In the blue corner:
The Colossal Monster of Cannot has no body,
became so fat with power
no skin could hold its all-consuming form.
But if it did have a face

that face would look like a melted
Ferrero Rocher.
Margaret Thatcher's face made out of melted
Ferrero Rocher.
Margaret Thatcher's face made out of melted
Ferrero Rocher,
excrement, lumpy porridge, vomit and spit.
It would look like Margaret Thatcher's face.

Julie Jones has a lovely face.
And lovely hands!
Far too elegant for hitting.
So what *is* the game plan her brain's knitting?

Born to a world that is brimful of *can't*,
Julie has always chosen to fight
with words as her war-paint and books as her shield.
But her tactics are far more than fistfuls of knowledge.
Julie knows the depth
of a walnut and orange sponge cake.
She sews the songs of Nick Cave into a salsa belly dance
that casts a chandelier of candles from India, out.
With the taste of South African choirs
baked in Manchester Tart,
it is Julie's gumption
that spark cracks The Colossal Monster back.
Whack!
Take that!
A *joie de vivre* attack!

Rrrrroll up! Rrrrroll up for the fight of the day,
the weeks, the decades,

we know this adversary can't be beaten
in three rounds.

Julie's taught generations to question *cannots*.
Students. Children. Grandchildren.
Julie teaches us that this Monster's ultimate downfall
will be its arrogant assumption
people like us won't aim higher.

From Uni she's retired, but Julie keeps inspiring;
keeps leading the like-minded to find all we've got
to keep challenging The Colossal Monster of Cannot,
and I believe Julie when she says we can win.

"We can outgrow anything we're told is our lot!"

The Myth of Protein

Biochemical compound
whose name Berzelius found.
Von Voit claimed, *"Flesh makes flesh."*
Sanger sequenced insulin,
Purutz prized haemoglobin
and the Swedish were impressed.

More studies on its benefits
directed mutagenesis
as Weissman had foreseen.
To give their claims such credence
does not distract from this grievance:
"Where do vegans *get protein?*

What exactly can *you eat?*
Can't be healthy, with no meat."
Such Shakespearian introspection.
Between the facts to delve,
lament, *"B12 or not B12,*
surely that *must be the question?"*

It's simple eating sensible.
The soy bean lacks cholesterol,
is easily fortified
and cooked can taste exceptional
(tongue-tinglingly sensual)
and, yes, it will provide

protein! (As will peanut butter,

black beans, flax seeds, pecans, almonds,
lentils and cashews),
and yet, here is *my* beef;
hearing debate on my *belief*,
people questioning what I *choose*.

I don't *choose* for pigs to feel.
Don't just *believe* their pain is real.
It's fact. Not myth. Not needed.
Can we, in evolution,
swap our myths for resolution,
see this cruelty superseded?

The fact's of proteins chemistry,
documents throughout history,
are laid out plain and clear,
but still, I hopefully wait
for that honest, heartfelt date
when protein's myths will finally
disappear.

A Vegan from Slough

A vegan called Jessie from Slough
tried hard to avoid any row,
but folk gave her grief,
said, *"Don't you miss beef?"*
She said, *"Not as much as the cow."*

A Vegan from Rochdale

A vegan called John from Rochdale
thought Gaga's meat-dress beyond t'pale,
so he said, *"Instead,*
I'll wear only bread."
His pants fell off when they went stale.

A Vegan from Torquay

A vegan called Jane from Torquay
kept playing her Thom Yorke CD,
but when her bloke longed
for a cheerier song
she switched over to Morrissey.

A Vegan from Round Here

A vegan called Jack from round here
said, *"I don't like being called 'queer'.*
I just love chickpeas
and tahini, so, please,
I'm a hummus-sexual, my dear."

Peace of Vegan Cake

Zen of cocoa.
Marzipan Mantra.
Sticky bowl of vanilla quiescence.

Cakes are forgiving.
Wooden spoon jerks:
soul stirring.
Self-raising spirits:
smooth as new found breath.

To be forgiving,
cream gritty sugar,
dissolve and flow
a consistent mixture.
Leave no crumbs or mess
anymore.

Jocelyn Brown, Jazz Cafe, Camden, 2008

Ear to ear, roof to floor,
the air's gone solid with bass
and the crowd has turned into liquid.
We've had to.
Everyone's melted into one sweaty, sing-a-long throng
bubbling song.
Simmering lips and shimmering hips slip slide between
the tightest slices of concrete sound.
Funk bound.
We are profound dancers, barely touch ground,
too important for 'ground'!
Jocelyn sings 'Keep On Jumping',
you and me, keep jumping,
my heart, you've tugged it to pieces,
when I jump, bits hit walls like jelly.
Splat!
Splish splash crash, our arms collide,
your tongue on mine.
Squish!

Time Travellers

for Rod, for all our wonderful years together xxxx

Time travel to our past,
Manchester, 2006.
I always wanted a man who could hold nails in his teeth
and you look dead sexy holding nails in your teeth.
You know how hammers work!
Understand screwdrivers!
Your arms, strong enough to lift me when
I fall apart in Tesco's, sat crying in the biscuit aisle,
my chewed up nails spiking teeth.
You're a man who can hold nails in his teeth,
but never tries to mend me.
I'll never make sense in the way a spirit level makes sense.
My wood and bubbles are all wrong.
Sometimes I'd love to twist how I stand,
pretend I'm right angles, proper straight,
but you love me crooked, weird and bent.
I do not look great with nails in my teeth...
but I do look dead sexy in fishnets!

Time travel to our present,
streets emptied, 2011,
time travel here.
You. Me.
Outside.
Yelling.
Broken words, broken yelling,
stupid words, breaking, not while I'm yelling!
My sentences are punctured, commas pus, I've severed colons...

I am talking shit.
You look like the sky, open, still.
Why was I yelling?
You used to be from Tunbridge Wells
but now we've rewritten our pasts
so I've known you since forever.
You tell me Tunbridge Wells would love a good yell,
to connect so heavy it hurts,
but it can't even touch without wincing;
Tunbridge Wells couldn't ever just let us be us,
all queer and sexy and yelling!
Hey!
Guess what?
We've yelled so hard
we've erased Tunbridge Wells from time and space!

One last time.
2040-something.
People say you look like Doctor Who so I know you can do this.
Tell me a queer might be Prime Minister
or that gays can now be gays on daytime TV.
Tell me that Tunbridge Wells can exist
if it wears a fez
and that supermarkets now have to have
designated areas for panic attacks,
little rooms where they play B-52's,
give you stuff to make out of glitter, Pritt Stick and potatoes.
Tell me we're together, old,
our love keeps regenerating and I will still have
...hair.
Immortal hair!
Tell me you'll love me beyond end of days and

I love you.
I love you!
Let's make this sci-fi epic love
where heroes will never die.

Purple

for a colour my colour-blindness has never let me see

Purple is there
making butterfly hands in an eye's corner,
in top hat shadows when you should be sleeping.
Smells of joss sticks and cold lakes.

Purple might be naked.
Off somewhere
with eye-liner swirls round large, flat nipples
and a moan like thunder stumbling
or
maybe strutting in straps of chiffon and velvet stripes
dancing down somebody else's street.

Lives in a handmade book
about eating disorders and lunar eclipses.
Did stop a boy from hanging himself.
Heard it's in diazepam and fairies.

Your imaginary friends might have liked Purple more than you.
Purple's nice to your Mum when you're not even there,
gets all scented oil and Stonehenge about it.
Didn't go to maths.
Blames dyspraxia and forests.

Purple is not 'no-trainers' clubs
or ironing.
Doesn't like meal deals
or long, ironic novels.

I think Purple was my first kiss
or
at least its memory.
Tasted like pumpkin seed,
black coffee,
skin bitten off round the nail.

When toddlers see ghosts it is Purple.

It is the language of time travel,
what's inside the sun,
inside your finger
and lips,
and Wizard's first brew of the day.

Sun

Sun grits teeth through centuries' shining.
Hates horizons.
Slaps hazy edges round another morning's corner,
yawns,
then with a wreak of curdled Milky Way
lets a long, helium fart
rip across the sky.

Storm clouds splutter,
their macho thunder turns to girly, gaseous squeaks.
Rainbows cackle,
call the storm clouds poofs,
make a spectacle of their tears.

Sun sighs.
Used to think being centre of everything would be
more than this.
Spent millennia fighting to be brightest,
best,
now feels ready to implode.

Resting elbows in the centre of a road,
hums a tune made from black holes and extinction.
Has everything.
Wants nothing
except, maybe, some time in the dark
or
just a day away from keeping up
horizons.

Hero

Once-upon-a-time, a barman worshipped the Sun.
Worked nights so didn't see much of it,
but in his head he'd got stories of the Fire God supreme,
Blaze Lord,
vanquishing monsters who'd eat out your dreams.

He called the Sun, *Hero*.
Believed it had six pairs of arms, giant wings of flame
and the handsomest nose in the galaxy.
Made moons blush and giggle their names.

His Sun was a Hero who rescued smiles
and fed them ideas 'til they were fat with luck.
Faster than a speeding comet,
could see around corners, rewrite destiny,
didn't break promises, could rewire a star.
Gave songs to orphans, faith to minstrels,
had the kind of hug you couldn't touch,
but kept, safe, underneath your skin.

Barman kept faith that Sun would come
one day,
teach him the Hero's Way.
He could be the Sun's wise-cracking sidekick.
Might even get his own light saber!
On long, lantern lit night shifts
washing drip trays,
watching drips
getting wasted,

barman believed that Sun would come.

Sun didn't break promises.

Hurrying home under a rejected moon,
he'd hum a tune made from
downing flagons and flying dragons,
race to his flat door.

At 4am every day
he'd get ready for bed,
each time dreaming he'd just stay awake
long enough to see
Sun.

Earth

If it could
this city would suckle the stars dry.
A colossal monster,
brick belly spreading,
puking out bin bags while still craving more.
This concrete cold parasite
is dead from the day down

while Rat holds up her dinner
like a tinfoil trophy,
trips a dapper tap dance
to melody of rain,

while Bumblebee chuckles
at Ant's impression of Adam,

while hurried Woodlouse pauses
to compliment Millipede's unshaved legs,

while sexy Snail flirting
so outrageously at parties,
known as Hermaphroditee,
trailing luscious mucus robes,
will call you Adonis,
will share the ditch ride home,
will whisper in the pavement cracks:

"You can have it all."

Snail

'When the rain calls Snail out
from sleepy, snail dreams,
sliding out a restful place
no human eye has seen,
silent Snail calls to rain:
"Let's wash this city clean!"...
Trail wraps the paving cracks
and litter in between.

Rain is calling Snail
through the greying of the street,
through a swollen puddle
stretching out its concrete seat,
to a green-red apple,
naked core torn indiscreet...
Apples travel half the world
to fall, crushed under feet.

I sit dry inside my flat
as Rain calls down to Snail.
People caught out in the storm
will curse the sleet and hail.
Flail back to brick high homes,
locked strong against the gale...
Back inside our big, brick shells,
so wrapped in our own trail.

Watch the green-red apple,
tender innards battered, split.

Watch as Snail passes by
beside the apple pip.
Easily killed. Its small life spilled
by just one similar hit...
I watch Snail brave the rain
from where I safely sit.'

4am

In the flat below mine
Wizard's sketching pictures
in gaps between ads, an old magazine.
Snail on his window ledge.
This is a 4am kind of magic
that only wizards and snails get.
Make Wizard some tea and
chat about the importance of kettles,
karma, Swanee kazoos, drawing cartoons
and watching a snail at 4am.
These are the little things we've got that make us
us.
We try to unbind ourselves from these hard back streets,
a city written with too much ink.
Paper-thin people fight to be rich
tearing themselves up,
outside.

Wizard

Wizard was first staged at Manchester's Contact on 25th May 2011. The show was researched, developed and written with an Arts Council England Grants for the Arts / National Lottery award and support from Manchester's Contact. The cast, in order of appearance, were:

WIZARD	Rod Tame
DAISUKE	Benny-Jo Zahl
MAN	Dominic Berry
URSULA	
MEDUSA	
DILLEN	Jo Warburton
A STRANGER	
THE ELDERS	Gerry Potter
Director	Martin 'Visceral' Stannage
Producer	Chris Jones

Wizard also received amazing support from the following people, all of whom receive my utmost thanks: Margaret, Dorothy and Business In The Arts Northwest; Anne-Marie and all at PANDA; Pete, Martin and all at Commonword / Cultureword; Jamie Winstanley and all at Gaydio; Ric Watts and all at Queer Up North; Richard and Mauro at Albino Mosquito; Neil and Matt at Chewing The Cud; Ian Wallis Photography; Chris Dommett; John McGrath; Liz O'Neill and Jo Bell.

SCENE ONE
'DEMON'

Spot light on WIZARD. He wears a dressing gown and has bare feet.

He stands by a battered armchair. On the chair is a magician's pointed hat. Around the chair are piles of envelopes, screwed up papers, packs of biscuits, two mugs, some jars of white pills, can of air-freshener, bottle of bleach, small cereal bowl, wooden spoon, tinsel, kettle and dish rack.

WIZARD:

Creep home,
keep alone down alley cracks,
deep hungry tracks, bones hollowed slack.
Where weeping clouds mourn bricked up back streets
funerals wait to attack.
Wide black sleepless eyes breathe whispered blinks.
Seeping bruises purple pinks.
The church tower sinks in a graveyard throne.
The last heir's breath - keep on.

There is a thin arm. Open hand.
Rat-tail fingers, money fanned.
Wants to soothe your aching heels,
he understands how your pain feels.
A careful grin on shadow's cheek
offers comfort - here's a seat.
Eyes talk beneath speech,
promising something... sweet.

Keep strong.
Walk on.
Watch toes
point home.
When your lonely
hopes start burning
cover your neck.
Resist the gloaming.

A thin arm stretched forward
could pull a faltering one toward
a gorge of claws - when sores sting sharp
that voice plucks like a distant harp.
That melody can hook in ears,
a life-choked memory reclears
of lidless love, not capped by fears.
A desperate smile appears

and with the hollow of tomorrow so far away,
the future can be forfeit for one happy today,
just one grain of colour in a desert of grey
and a curse of *'Come what may!'*
This Demon, waiting for the meek,
will promise anything you seek,
knows all the perfect words to speak -
but show him you're not weak!

Keep strong. Walk on.
Eyes wrapped round the road home.
Keep going. Never drop.
Stop lonely hopes from growing.
Keep strong. Walk on.

Eyes wrapped round the road home.
Keep going. Never drop.
Keep wing-clipped feet from slowing.

Keep strong.
Walk on.
Get home.
Stay home.
When your lonely
hopes start burning
cover your neck.
Resist the gloaming.

A deep voice, seemingly from nowhere, suddenly booms out across the room.

DAISUKE THE DISH RACK [VOICE-OVER]:

Wizard loses 13 hit points.
Wizard gains 3 experience points.

Spot switches off WIZARD.

SCENE TWO
THE FIRST DAY

Second spot lights up on other side of stage.

A MAN enters and walks into new spot. MAN wears shirt / tie, trousers, smart shoes. He has his mobile phone and some poems in his pocket.

This side of the stage is MAN's office where his office chair and laptop live.

Mind numbing elevator music begins to play.

MAN begins his normal, boring day at work. Repetitive motions - type, take call, drink tea, type, take call, drink tea...

Spot off MAN and back up on WIZARD. WIZARD, now wearing his hat, has a collection of jars and liquids. He starts to have a great time creating spells.

As music plays, spot now alternates between the two - MAN, bored at work, repeating same actions, while WIZARD grows increasingly excited with his spell's progress.

Music fades.

SCENE THREE
'PLAYING MORTAL KOMBAT'

The working day is at its end, but MAN is still in his office after all his colleagues have gone home. He pulls a scruffy piece of paper from his pocket. He starts practicing a poem.

MAN:

This is a... no, no, um... *this* is a, er...

MAN puts paper back in pocket, clears throat and starts again.

This is an age of caged hostility
where Health & Safety forms and files
fry brains,
pry pains,
our supposed source of security sees highs waned
and lives drained.
Cries contained can't scream through offices,
can't rip through orifices,
can't express a desk job's bubbling hate,
hurt
and harm,

but playing Mortal Kombat guarantees you inner calm.

Playing Mortal Kombat guarantees your inner calm.
Maybe play as Jax where you can tear off someone's arm.
Perform an 'Organ Donor' - crush a heart inside your palm...
Playing Mortal Kombat guarantees your inner calm.

Insurance claims and tax returns incite most deadly vows
but Sonya Blade's leg toss can never fail to arouse.
Funding forms leave hair-lines torn - make us curse and hiss.
Sub Zero's spinecord rip will induce instant love and bliss.
Baraka's blades decapitate with almost cheeky charm.
Playing Mortal Kombat guarantees your inner calm.

Without Mortal Kombat I'd have murdered half my school
and every boss I've ever had - fatality by duel,
but Mortal Kombat soothed my wrath, I felt my fury fade.
Let us respect its full effect with a worldwide parade!

Let's sing of Queen Sindel in hymns, perhaps we'll pen a
psalm,
"Playing Mortal Kombat Guarantees Your ... ..."

If life's been hard, left you scarred, here's a healing balm.
Playing Mortal Kombat guarantees your inner calm.

MAN, pleased with his rehearsal, turns and exits.

SCENE FOUR
'THE ELDERS' SONG'

Full light up on WIZARD's flat. WIZARD is now calmly sat in his chair.

WIZARD:

Brew for me a cuppa tea
and fill to brim my mug.
Warm our bodies, brains and speech -
internal, liquid hug...

Ah! Good morrow, good morrow, my fairest, most rotund Ursula.

WIZARD holds up the kettle. The kettle talks cheerfully back to him.

URSULA THE KETTLE [VOICE-OVER]:

And a shamanic morning to you, good sir.

WIZARD:

Oh, Ursula, Ursula, spherical Ursula! May all your tea be brown and bountiful this brilliant, beautiful day.

URSULA THE KETTLE [V/O]:

Oh, sir, you make me blush!

WIZARD:

Another hot flush? Not unusual in a kettle. But don't call me 'sir'.

URSULA THE KETTLE [V/O]:

Then please, tell us your name! All we've ever had the pleasure of knowing, sir, is your kind... noble... handsome face.

WIZARD:

Oh, stop, stop, stop! You flatter me! Ursula, *you* are a kettle. *You* have a name. *I* am a Wizard. *I* do not want to be known by a name. A name is a powerful thing.

DAISUKE THE DISH RACK [V/O]:

A successful counter.
Wizard earns 5 experience points.

WIZARD:

Thank you, Daisuke. Very observant.

URSULA THE KETTLE [V/O]:

Daisuke, take all my 'hit points' now if it makes you happy. I never asked to play your silly game.

WIZARD:

None of us did, Ursula, yet here we all... are...

WIZARD pauses and then rushes over to one audience member in front row.

By the Goddess! Look... at... you...! How could I have babbled on for so long before our eyes so gently met? My dear, my dear, my dear, I don't want to be rude but you could not look worse if you'd just found the pus-eating crater demons of Saturn's rings copulating in your cornflakes. Don't you think, Ursula?

URSULA THE KETTLE [V/O]:

Truly a face only a carpet goblin could love.

WIZARD turns to another audience member.

WIZARD:

Are you responsible for this one? You are now. Group love, nurturing, male bonding, full body contact, all that. You will do a wonderful job, too, I feel it in my wizardy waters. I can sense you have skilful fingers - we wizards know such things, it's like a ninety-eighth sense. You'll be magnificent!

Back to first person.

Would you like a drink? Tea? Peppermint? Hot water with a slice of lemon? By the Goddess, you should have whatever you want in life my dear do not let anyone get in your way. You!

WIZARD points to another, different audience member

Whatever this creature demands of you, see that it's every whim, fancy, craving and fetish are satisfied, whatever it takes. The carpet must stay aligned - such is the way the shagpile blows. Excuse me.

WIZARD rushes off stage.

Silence.

URSULA THE KETTLE [V/O]:

Don't mind him, love. He's a sandwich short of a picnic. Bless.

WIZARD hurries back on with a drink he hands to the first audience member.

WIZARD:

Hydrate, my dear, hydrate and be free! Free! Look at you! Gods and Goddesses of the carpet. Don't you think, Daisuke?

DAISUKE THE DISH RACK [V/O]:

Carpet Goblin drinks Wizard's elixir.
Carpet Goblin regains 12 hit points.

WIZARD:

My dears, I have penned a passionate homage to the truly exquisite wonder that is Wizard's elixir, the humble teabag.

We would love to share it with you now if that's OK? And if you felt inclined to burst into spontaneous, rapturous applause at its climax, well, that would be lovely too. Are we ready? Splendid!

Brew for me a cuppa tea
and fill to brim my mug.

URSULA THE KETTLE [V/O]:

Warm our bodies, brains and speech -
internal, liquid hug.

WIZARD:

Every word I form
began an undug thought to free,
each like an acorn in my skull
to feed and wet with tea.
You and me, together—

> *WIZARD is interrupted as MAN enters his flat. MAN holds an envelope.*

MAN:

Hey. You busy?

WIZARD:

Oh! Hello, hello, hello! Not at all, come on in, look at my carpet!

MAN:

Can't stop. Just saw this letter for you downstairs and thought it looked important.

WIZARD:

Right, right - listen to this - Brew for me a cuppa tea and fill to brim my mug—

MAN:

Sorry mate, I really can't stop.

WIZARD:

Won't take long - Warm our bodies, brains and speech—

MAN:

No, really. I'll call round tomorrow after work, bring your shopping round. OK?

WIZARD:

My carpet might not be so full tomorrow.

MAN:

Well, I'm sorry mate, but I have to go. Have a good night, yeah?

MAN hands WIZARD envelope and exits. WIZARD is disorientated.

WIZARD:

Oh. Where was I?

WIZARD looks at first audience member again.

How's your drink, my dear? It's clearly done you good, you look ten times the wilted, slime-encrusted hobgoblin you were before supping that. Don't you think, Ursula?

URSULA THE KETTLE [V/O]:

Ten times, sir.

WIZARD:

Ten times. Can I just ask, how many of you here are in love? I am sensing a lot of love. Please, raise a paw or hoof or talon or whatever you feel appropriate if you are in love. Oh! It is the most wonderful feeling, isn't it? See, Daisuke doesn't understand. Dish racks don't. Sure, he once slew the dragon of Balgaku (armed with nothing but a bent fork and a brillo) but... ask him about love... nothing.

DAISUKE THE DISH RACK [V/O]:

Daisuke successfully evades attack.

WIZARD:

Exactly. I tell you, you will find no greater love in life than the love of a kettle. Ursula, Ursula, Ursula, you deserve centre stage for this, my sweet.

WIZARD fetches kettle, kisses it and then gives it to someone in audience.

URSULA THE KETTLE [V/O]:

Oh, thank you, sir.

WIZARD:

We have yet another new friend here, Ursula. We must not forget manners.

WIZARD starts to open letter.

URSULA THE KETTLE [V/O]:

Oh, no! Sir, please don't—

A menacing soundscape of tortured screams and howls pours from the envelope. WIZARD drops envelope in fright. It stops screaming. Hesitantly, WIZARD prods it with his foot, opens it just a little with his toe. The soundscape roars again and WIZARD hides behind his chair. The soundscape builds into a collective of voices calling to WIZARD. As they speak, WIZARD slowly crawls out from behind the chair and approaches the envelope.

THE ELDERS [VOICE-OVER]:

Dear Mister... insert-name-in-this-space.
We are writing to conclude on your case.
You are not... 'ill'... These words are misplaced.
Sometimes we all get a little sad.
Yours isn't the only form we've had.

Lose that frown and dressing gown.
Let's get our statistics down.
Hey, hey, hey! Earn your play!
Live to work another day.

You say you're too ill to go outside.
We said where therapists were. We tried!
You wouldn't go! You just stayed inside!
Have you thought we might suspect your sneaking?
Is this just attention seeking?

You said you 'panic'. We heard your call.
With our pills, you'd feel nothing at all.
You wouldn't take them! Of all the gall!
Have you thought we might suspect your faking
easy way of money making?

Lose that frown and dressing gown.
Let's get our statistics down.
We'll clear up all this mess and fuss
though no-one ever says thanks to us.

WIZARD:

I said I would work. I'd work from home.
I'd work quite happily left on my own.

THE ELDERS [V/O]:

Well, how could you find work with that tone?
Have you thought about our budget's cuts?
Now, please, no more 'ifs' and 'buts',

lose that frown and dressing gown.
Let's get our statistics down.
Hey, hey, hey! Earn your play!
Live to work another day.

Lose that frown and dressing gown.
Let's get our statistics down.
We'll clear up all this mess and—

> *They are cut off mid-sentence as WIZARD picks up envelope
> and tears it up. Shaken, he reclaims kettle from audience and
> climbs up onto his chair.*
>
> *Black out.*

SCENE FIVE
THE SECOND DAY

Lights up on WIZARD now sat calmly on his chair wrapping his kettle in tinsel. MAN is now also in his flat, unpacking a bag of shopping as he speaks.

MAN:

So, they put all the poets on right after some awful stand up. Proper bad. No one got it and half the audience left before I got on. I was last poet on too, place was empty. And I'd got 'Mortal Kombat' word perfect and everything. Bastards.

WIZARD:

Pointless pretenders. Forget these stupid human words!

MAN notices there are envelopes on the floor.

MAN:

Hey, you haven't opened these yet. They could be urgent. Some long lost uncle might've died, left you a multi-millionaire!

MAN hands WIZARD envelopes. WIZARD freezes. The soundscape of tortured screams kicks in.

THE ELDERS [V/O]:

Dear Mister... insert-name-in-this-space—

Unseen by MAN, WIZARD rips them in two and tosses them over his shoulder. The soundscape and voices are immediately cut off mid-flow. MAN continues, oblivious to what has just happened.

MAN:

Did you know you were out of teabags? Mate, how've *you* made it through a whole day with no tea? Well, I know you hate posh muck but I was feeling a bit 'exotic' today so I have bought us... Yorkshire Tea!

WIZARD:

Ursula the kettle said
her work-wear makes her blue
so I wrap her up in tinsel
every time she makes a brew.

MAN:

Well, Yorkshire Tea was cheapest. I think you'll think it's good.

WIZARD:

Oh, slice mine eyes with salted razors,
devils black my blood!

MAN:

So, that's a no to Yorkshire Tea? My Dad reckons it's nice.

WIZARD:

Then wrench thy Father's wretched lips,
force-feed him worms and lice.

MAN:

Hm. Given half the chance...

*MAN goes to WIZARD's kitchen, collecting kettle from him as
he passes.*

You know you've only powder left for one more laundry load?

WIZARD:

Pray... Demon Moon... engulfing skies
like nipples... on a toad.

MAN:

Yeah... So, my day. You wouldn't believe how my boss spoke
to me.
No respect. Told me off! I was just making tea!

MAN leaves kettle, rejoins WIZARD.

Hey! See what I did there? Me / tea? Freestyle rhyming! Eh, it's
catching!
And... I've got more rhymes hatching!

MAN is very pleased with himself. WIZARD just rolls his eyes.

If you had heard my boss today -
my God, she went ballistic.
Hm... Ballistic... Holistic? Sadistic? Statistic? ...Statistic!
If you had heard my boss today -
my God, she went ballistic.
Didn't treat me like a man -
more like a—

> WIZARD interrupts, lifts pack of biscuits from side of chair,
> offers it to MAN.

WIZARD:

Chocolate biscuit?

> MAN frowns, does not take one. WIZARD smiles, takes one
> for himself.

She doust you dark with harpy tongue,
in virgin sweat, still warm?

MAN:

Worse than that.
She made me fill a Health & Safety form.
I hadn't Risk Assessed
the boiling water in my cup.

WIZARD:

I care not for these 'forms' or 'risk',
this wisdom down-side-up.

WIZARD rises from his chair, starts to head off.

MAN:

Well nor do I, mate. Fill a form
just to brew up? It's mad!
But hey, don't go, that's not the half,
my day got way more bad.

WIZARD stops, turns and gives MAN a disapproving stare.

What?

WIZARD:

"Day... got way more bad." *Really*?

MAN:

What? Just freestyling.

WIZARD:

Far greater things betray this Earth
than in your office dwells.
I've dragons in my bookcase...
and their teats won't milk themselves.
Your boss! Your boss! Her lore fixates
yet could she matter less?
Is she dragon? Is she demon?
Is she gargoyle?

MAN:

Yes!

WIZARD:

She... *is*... gargoyle? Troll... of stone?
That's what you're saying to me?

MAN:

She... *is*... a gargoyle... wings of rock...
no crueller beast there be.
Her claws a-craggy, jaws a-droolin'
sulphur, eyes wild.
I must feed her forms or else...
she'll eat my first born child.

WIZARD nods, goes to fetch the kettle.

WIZARD:

By the Goddess. I know spells
that crumble gargoyle gall.
Carve some woodchip! Melt some mould!
This gargoyle leech *will* fall!
My mightiest magic I'll gift you,
our fiercest rage she'll see...
but first - a cuppa!

MAN:

That sounds pukka,
but we've only Yorkshire Tea.

WIZARD gasps, puts down kettle.

WIZARD:

OK. *I'll* go.

MAN:

You'll go?

WIZARD:

I'll go.

MAN:

You what?

WIZARD:

You heard! *I'll* go...

Snap *Click* *Thwack!*
My heart armour... is intact.

MAN:

Mission target sighted!

WIZARD:

There is *no* turning back...
This is a quest to retrieve
the most awesome treasure

MAN:

most power-reaping life spark!

WIZARD:

Yet most quiescent pleasure.
For its lure, a king could murder,

MAN:

forsake riches, live in rags!

WIZARD:

Its legend is sung in many land's tongue.

MAN:

The *magic* of...

MAN & WIZARD TOGETHER:

> *Teabags!* <

MAN:

Though square bags suffice,
the mystic pyramid's our target.

WIZARD:

Tea will save if we can brave the trials of...

MAN:

...Supermarket...

WIZARD:

O... ...Supermarket,
where the happiest heart could crack.
For tea, I don my heart armour,
Snap *Click* *Thwack!*
O... ...Supermarket,
enslaves her workers' dreams.
Promised opportunity.
Most will never leave.

Supermarket spares her drones
a few loose pennies to hold
whilst hoarding for herself
piles of diamonds, rubies, gold.
Supermarket's clones accept,
blind follow their leader's call.
If they didn't take her pennies,
well... they might get nothing at all.

Their withering queen, deflowering thought,
dictates when they should eat,
when they should rest, when they should smile,
free will is obsolete.
That isn't life.
These drones exist in undead stagnancy.
Their stares en-flare fears I can't share...
I just want to buy tea.

WIZARD has panic attack. He falls back onto his chair. He starts trembling, cannot breathe, his body all heart palpitations and chest pains. He gets hot flashes, cold flashes, sweats, feels nauseous, dizzy and clasps at his own throat. WIZARD believes he is going to die.

WIZARD:

I just want to buy tea.
I just want to buy tea.
I just want to buy tea.
I just want to buy tea.
I just want to buy tea.
I just want to buy tea.
I just want to buy tea.
I just want to buy tea.
I just want to buy tea.
I just want to buy tea.

MAN:

It's OK. You don't have to go anywhere. You're all right. Just breathe into it. One- two- one- two- one- two...

After some time WIZARD regains control of his breathing.

WIZARD:

Friend. Hero. Valiant knight.
Heart firm as metal.
Survive these Supermarket ghouls...
and I'll put on the kettle.

MAN nods and exits.

URSULA THE KETTLE [V/O]:

Um... Forgive me, sir, but can your friend really succeed in his quest unaided? With all your power, sir, I can't help but feel that we really should be—

WIZARD:

By the Goddess, Ursula... You... are... right...

DAISUKE THE DISH RACK [V/O]:

Wizard levelled up!
Strength increase by 3 points.
Wizard taught Man new spell:
SUPERMARKET-NINJA-KICK-ASS-GOD-DEMON-
VAMPIRE-KING...
Level 1.

16 bit video game music starts to play as WIZARD bellows into the air.

WIZARD:

Steel your nerve adventurer,
be dexterous and wise.

URSULA THE KETTLE [V/O]:

Make haste to Supermarket...

WIZARD:

Tea bags are aisle five.

URSULA THE KETTLE [V/O]:

There's a milk spill, aisle three!

WIZARD:

A fat white ocean wide.
Steer your trolley deftly lest

WIZARD & URSULA THE KETTLE [V/O]:

you wake the gremlin inside!

WIZARD:

Should your trolley veer harsh left
you've just upset its gremlin.
I gift to you one SLEEPWAX spell
to soothe those wheels a-trembling.

URSULA THE KETTLE [V/O]:

Beyond baked bean tin avalanche,
behold our goal - tea!

WIZARD:

But yet, beware the check out tills,
sat there are sisters three.

DAISUKE THE DISH RACK [V/O]:

First gorgon attack!

MEDUSA [VOICE-OVER]:

Would you like to buy a loyalty card, love?

MAN [VOICE-OVER]:

No thanks.

DAISUKE THE DISH RACK [V/O]:

Man successfully evades attack.
Man earns 15 experience points.
Excellent!

WIZARD:

Supermarket gorgons,
hook-clawed nails forebode.
Spit fire if you pay with change
or buy food with no barcode.
I swear to you - one look could kill!
O mortal man-hate frown.
So judging should you shop barefoot
or in your dressing gown.

DAISUKE THE DISH RACK [V/O]:

Man raises The Wallet of Shangranoogah.
Unleashes The Ten Pound Note of Galbooshvangarooh.

MAN [V/O]:

You got change for a tenner?

DAISUKE THE DISH RACK [V/O]:

A stunning attack!
First gorgon loses 12 hit points.

MEDUSA [V/O]:

Yeah. Here's your change, love. Night.

DAISUKE THE DISH RACK [V/O]:

First gorgon is destroyed!
Man earns 100 experience points.

WIZARD:

Whispering 'Weird!' and 'Paranoid!'
with spindly fingery glee.

URSULA THE KETTLE [V/O]:

Who can survive such deathly foes

WIZARD:

to bring back milk and tea?

Music ends.

DAISUKE THE DISH RACK [V/O]:

Game auto saving... Auto save complete.

MAN re-enters holding another carrier bag containing tea and some Marmite.

WIZARD:

Hark! So quick?

MAN:

I took the bus.

WIZARD gives MAN a sharp look.

I mean.... rode dragon back!

WIZARD:

I sense gorgon guard lives still.
You fear her next attack.

MAN:

What gorgon guard?

WIZARD:

That devil beast.

MAN:

The check-out girl?

WIZARD:

The snake!

MAN:

Don't call her that. That isn't nice.

WIZARD:

So 'nice' your soul she'll take.

MAN:

She's just a girl. Just bored. Not bad.
Her name is Claire.

WIZARD:

Untrue! Your bag has touched Medusa's claw!
Her septic residue.

MAN:

No, that's just my Marmite.
Look... Medusa's... not after my soul.

WIZARD:

You side with the outsiders,
see you switch from pole to pole.
No - hush your heathen, howling tongue
that knows not friend or foe.
Dismiss our wisdom, side with her,
some witch you hardly know.

MAN:

Hey, I'm not taking sides, I'm only saying—

WIZARD:

Yes, we hear.
Some loyalty to Wizard's
far too much to ask, we fear.
That's why those words you say you craft
are feeble. Lifeless. Lame.
Those eyes can't tell what's truth therefore
your words suffer the same.
To capture passion, pain or spark
the scribe must stay alert.
You've never known true torment,
yet pretend you've been so hurt.
This speak of 'Mortal Kombat',
clucking tongue of—

MAN:

Right. You've made your point. You're the one with all the
fucking pain and magic and spark and I know fuck all. I don't
have to listen to this.

WIZARD:

Dismiss our wisdom.

MAN starts to leave and then turns back.

MAN:

You know what, with all your magical powers you can't get
your head out your own arse.

MAN exits.

SCENE SIX
'SPIRITS'

Lights dim to just spotlight on WIZARD. Once again, the soundscape of tortured screams calls, this time from the torn papers on the floor.

THE ELDERS [V/O]:

Dear Mister... insert-name-in-this-space-

WIZARD drops to his knees, tears up the papers. Voices and soundscape stop.

WIZARD addresses the audience.

WIZARD:

The soul of an ancient eight-armed ninja
drag-queen dragon-king
is locked inside my shower
and joins in when I sing.
Sometimes we dissect biscuits,
wonder why the sky's so long.
Yes, I go in naked.
Nothing sexual's going on.

My Hoover says I'm lying
when I beg him not to clean
because I swear there's goblins
in my carpet he's not seen.
I say, *"They put the milk back
in the fridge when we forget!"*
but drag-queen dragon-king and Hoover
don't believe me yet.

Spot out. Second spot up on MAN's office. MAN is pacing up and down.

MAN:

Panic will not understand
my cousin's wife's Sunday dinner etiquette
or what hands ought to do in interviews
or how to talk to friends of friends' Dads.
Panic's clumsy. Breaks things.

Spot switches off MAN as first spot again lights up WIZARD.

WIZARD:

Ursula the kettle says:

URSULA THE KETTLE [V/O]:

My work-wear makes me blue.

WIZARD:

So I wrap her up in tinsel
every time she makes a brew.

URSULA THE KETTLE [V/O]:

I never met a human
on this Earth or anywhere
who every time they make the tea
puts tinsel in their hair.

Spot out on WIZARD and up on MAN.

MAN:

Sometimes *my* body falls into itself.
My heart starts to... throat-slap,
flap like dying fish,
tastes like... grated carrot in sawdust.
Tastes like fists in my neck.
Eyes kick inside lids,
steel tear-capped kicks.

While 'real' folk clump round in size nine realities.
'Real' folk. Big, ugly feet.
Some people's ideas look like feet.
Feet without souls!
Stuffed deep in sock, hidden ugly.
Too repressed to know Panic
if it bit them on the brain.

Both spots now on. WIZARD starts to get angry.

MAN: ### WIZARD:

They're just husks of mortgage.
Sudoku stained.
I don't have feet   My Hoover says I'm lying when I
or anything ugly.   beg him not to clean.
I am the subtext of wordless night,   He ought to know
the blinding light   there's goblins in
of total darkness.   my carpet he's not seen.
See, they can't hold down the sky. See, they can't see what matters,

Pulled out of body,
free of frenzied skin,
bound only to bone by
the thinnest of truths,
I'm a weightless parade
wrapped round
a sunbeam guiding my body home.

caught up in the city drone.
There's shelves of elves in sequined bells
hop-scotching here at home.
The thinnest of truths
binds the moon to oceans,
Sun to Earth.
We're rock unsolid fantasy,
know what magic's worth.
Everything we need is here.
Fantastic, roof to floor!
Nothing outside this flat matters.

Spot switches off WIZARD.

SCENE SEVEN
THE THIRD DAY

The sound of a mobile phone ringtone, 'The Wonderful Wizard of Oz', plays. MAN gets out phone from his pocket.

MAN:

Hello? Yes? Oh... Yes... Sure... Definitely! Thank you! Cheers!

The same elevator music from the start of the show plays.

MAN goes about his normal day at work. As before - type, take call, drink tea, type, take call, drink tea... but this time he is much cheerier.

Spot switches off MAN and back onto WIZARD.

WIZARD is in his flat gathering together a pile of envelopes. He is very angry. The odd snatch of broken dialogue from THE ELDERS can be heard mixed into the elevator music. Each time they speak, WIZARD flinches.

The spots continue to alternate - MAN even happier at work, repeats same actions with added gusto. WIZARD grows increasingly angry, grabs one envelope and tears it in half.

MAN exits. WIZARD starts manically tearing up all the papers around him.

Music ends as WIZARD is completely surrounded by torn papers.

SCENE EIGHT
'SHAPE-SHIFTER' / 'IMP OR GIANT'

Full lights up on WIZARD's flat. WIZARD addresses audience.

WIZARD:

I could crush you with one foot. If I was wearing my dragon-skin stilettos now, by the Goddess, it would hurt. Look at yourselves, squirming round my carpet, stealing crumbs you think I drop. You're all thieves. You don't own anything - you steal. No one owns anything anyway, just whoever's biggest and loudest crushes those smaller. Well, I'm biggest here. I have never dropped a crumb and I'm watching you, so don't steal anything. All this is mine.

MAN enters wearing jeans / T-shirt. He holds a cat basket.

MAN:

Mate, I've had some great news. But I've got a massive favour to ask. This guy at work has called in sick. He was meant to be going to this big, posh hotel tonight so that he could attend some conference thing tomorrow morning. They've asked me to go instead! They never offer me nothing! I mean, the conference itself sounds a load of shite but I'll get mega brownie points for saving the day. It's just one night away but - well, I got no-one to look after Dillen have I?

WIZARD:

Dillen?

MAN:

Dillen.

WIZARD:

What... is 'Dillen'?

MAN:

Dillen! My cat! I told you when I found him stray—

WIZARD:

No time! No time for that!

MAN:

Oh, come on, mate, it's just one night,
he could stay here - no sweat.
Look, I've had Dillen eight months now,
it's high time you two met.

WIZARD:

Please... you're no good at spontaneous rhyme.

MAN:

You'd be asleep most of the time,
it's only a few hours.
I can't just leave him on his own...
him and his... 'magic powers'.

WIZARD:

By the Goddess... You say you've nurtured this... creature... for
eight lunar cycles?

MAN:

Winter sun turned its back on our buried horizon
strangled by snow.
Some froze. Some shattered.

A small Shape-Shifter was searching for shelter.

He looked like a kitten,
ginger paws shivering, eyes quivering blue.
Cold as silence hollowed to the core,
alone, a lost meow.
He looked like a cat,
face framed in frost, until
he started shifting his shape,

more armour than armadillo!
He became a tortoise-like shield,
rhinoceros-rough,
deflected blizzards, deflected sleet,
he deflected destiny to keep himself alive

so he did survive when nights enlarged
and clouds storm clattered.
Though Shape-Shifter's shield was battered and soaked
he was not broken. He had...

WIZARD:

...hope.

MAN:

...Hope... he would meet a wise man... or wizard...
someone in the know
with their own warm magic,
watch fur orange glow.
Hope he would again shift his shape, past castaway
to play,
transform into monkey,
a ginger jester clowning round chair legs—

WIZARD:

—summersault chasing his tail!

MAN:

More leap than frog!

WIZARD:

More song than bird!

MAN:

His loud meow proudly heard,
he knew would fill this new found home... one day.
Shape-Shifter kept believing his lonely cold would end.

WIZARD:

There is magic out there.

MAN:

Shape-Shifter knew that one day he would meet
a friend.

*MAN puts his hand on WIZARD's shoulder. WIZARD sighs
heavily.*

WIZARD:

One night.

MAN:

One night! I will repay you, mate,
I don't know how.
I promise, Dillen is no fuss.
You're no fuss, right?

DILLEN:

Meow!

MAN laughs and exits.

DAISUKE THE DISH RACK [V/O]:

Dillen levelled up!
Dillen cast
CAT-STINK-FART

level 929.
Wizard is engulfed in thick, toxic gas.
Wizard loses 56 hit points...

URSULA THE KETTLE [V/O]:

Sir, look out! That noxious cloud - a derrière brigand has formed from Shape-Shifter's bum!

WIZARD:

By the Goddess! A back-passage spectre... Grade 8! Daisuke, level me up!

DAISUKE THE DISH RACK [V/O]:

Wizard levelled up!
Daisuke taught Wizard new spell:
FABREEZE OF DOOM...
Level 6.

WIZARD:

Take cover, Shape-Shifter! Have at thee, bottom-behemoth!

WIZARD casts spell on the gaseous monster, dances round with arms in air.

DAISUKE THE DISH RACK [V/O]:

A stunning attack!
Back-passage spectre loses 83 hit points.
Back-passage spectre... is destroyed!
Wizard earns nine million experience points!

URSULA THE KETTLE [V/O]:

You did it, sir! You saved us all!

WIZARD:

Wizard wins. Flawless victory.

There is a knock at the door.

WIZARD:

Oh hark, you come to take it back,
this beast with devil's arse!
Why'd you knock, you never kno—

A STRANGER [VOICE-OVER]:

Hello, Mr Clark. Can I come in?

WIZARD:

Who are you?

A STRANGER [V/O]:

I came to see you before, Mr Clark. About a year ago? Did you
get my letter?

*A STRANGER enters. STRANGER wears smart, office clothes
and carries a file.*

A STRANGER:

It's all right, Mr Clark. I'd just like to ask you some questions. Can I come in?

WIZARD:

I don't know.

A STRANGER:

Oh, Mr Clark, is that your cat?

WIZARD:

No.

A STRANGER:

I do love cats. Can I stroke her? Is that all right, if I come in and stroke your cat?

WIZARD:

Um... Yeah? He... farts a lot.

A STRANGER:

Oh. She looks well. Adorable. Aren't you just adorable? Mr Clark, you're doing very well. Can you wash yourself, Mr Clark?

WIZARD:

Sorry?

A STRANGER:

Can you wash yourself, Mr Clark? Do you brush your own teeth? Do you comb your own hair? Do you wash your own clothes... or not?

WIZARD:

Um... Yes?

A STRANGER:

So, you *can* wash yourself, Mr Clark. That's good. Very good. Now, our records say that you still don't believe you can go outside. Why is that?

WIZARD:

Wh... what?

A STRANGER:

What is it, Mr Clark, that makes you think you can't go outside?

WIZARD:

Outside is bad.

A STRANGER:

Bad. It's... bad? OK. I'll just write that down in your file, Mr Clark. 'Bad'... Mr Clark, could you please tell me what happened when you did last go outside?

WIZARD:

I said. It was bad.

A STRANGER:

Help me understand. What could be too bad for a Wizard?

WIZARD:

I was sat alone when I saw it.
In the bar's safe corner where no-one else sits.
Away from the giants, their laughter like grit.
Away from catty dwarves' cruel chitter-chat-chit.
Away from wafer thin willo-the-wisps
fingering magazines between vodka sips.
I chewed my shaking nails like half-eaten bags of crisps
watching this cackling, barefoot Imp.

I watched it. Barefoot. Waving its shoes.
Acting like it invented feet.
Cackling up to the jukebox din
through the crowd so thick with their talk so thin.
No-one else gave it a glance.
Sheltered behind my fat finger mask,
I thought, *"One- two- one- two- one- breathe,"*
turned my ears from its barefoot beat.

Imp flitted forward, cheeks and teeth,
elbows jabbed a staccato jig.
Too wrapped up in its own bare feet,
accidentally... knocked over
...a Giant's... full
...drink

Smash!

Giant's face... engorged.
Cherry red... eyes glacéd.
Lager danced down his mountainous shirt,
rumbaed to the valley of his lap.
Giant's knuckle hair rose like spears.
Imp - bare-faced - had no fears.
I thought, *"One- two- one- two- one- breathe."*
My fingers hugged my beer and I felt myself freeze.

Drenched and deranged, Giant leapt with a roar,
slammed down fists, a fight, or more
and Imp... waltzed away,
oblivious... free.
Seemingly unseen,
grinned relentlessly.
The crowd hadn't flinched, their natter still bobbing along.
Giant sat down. The night sailed on.

"One- two- one—" I still could see
Giant's massive muscle, Imp's barefoot glee.
In my safe bar corner where no-one else breathes
the air got sticky like someone spilled the breeze.
I thought, *"One- two- one- two—"* to ease,
bit nails deep, tasted them bleed,
Panic attacked on the count of *"Three..."*

I would do anything to be bigger
or smaller
than me.

A STRANGER:

OK. I believe that you believe that is true. I believe something different. I believe that you saw an argument and that that made you feel a bit upset. It's OK to feel a bit upset. There is nothing wrong with feeling a bit upset. Sometimes, everybody feels a bit upset. That's normal. I know a man you could talk to about these 'imps' and 'giants'. How would that make you feel?

Lights grow dimmer. Spot on WIZARD.

WIZARD:

How I... feel? Where... to begin?
Sharp as light, you think me dim.
Came to curse yet call me kin?
Lies too fat. Veils too thin.
My sin? I hate your heavenly grin.
You'd cast me out, let demons pin
me down, rip me limb from limb.
So I must beg... to stay in.

Beg you... while you smile and sit.
Beg you... *"Save me from the pit*
where demons bit and hit and slit!"
Beg you... ...I'm not doing it.
May plagues of locusts' swarming din
and storms of blood rain grip you grim!
I spite your life from soul to brim!
I will *not* beg! So...
you win.

Full lights on WIZARD's flat.

A STRANGER:

Mr Clark? Did you hear what I said? I asked how you would
feel if I—

WIZARD:

My name's not 'Clark'. I don't have a name.

A STRANGER:

I'm sorry, Mr Clark, I can't hear what you're—

WIZARD:

Yes. Yes, I'll... talk to your... man.

A STRANGER:

Lovely. Now, Mr Clark, I just need you to sign here...

Black out. STRANGER exits.

Fast, loud, angry, instrumental music plays.

*In the darkness, WIZARD knocks over his chair. There is
sound of tearing paper and things being upturned.*

Music ends.

SCENE NINE
THE FOURTH DAY

Lights up on WIZARD on upturned chair.

URSULA THE KETTLE [V/O]:

The soul of an ancient eight-armed ninja
drag-queen dragon-king
is locked inside my shower
and joins in when I sing.
Sometimes we dissect biscuits—

WIZARD:

By the Goddess! Ursula, hush your ridiculous bubbling before
I break your nozzle off and feed you to the Moon Demons.

Silence.

DAISUKE THE DISH RACK [V/O]:

Ursula... You all right?

URSULA THE KETTLE [V/O]:

Yes, Daisuke. Thank you.

*WIZARD leaps to his feet, picks up the kettle and slams it
against the ground.*

WIZARD:

Curse by hail-storm! Curse by fire-spawn! Curse by thunder
and malice!

Silence.

WIZARD sits back down.

MAN enters in shirt / tie. He's got more envelopes.

MAN:

Well, how are my two favourite guys—

MAN stops as he notices all the paper... and cat poo in the middle of the room.

Oh my God. What's that?

WIZARD:

It's... an orb... from Goddess fire.

MAN:

It's poo. It's from the cat.
Where is Dillen? Have you fed him?
Fuck, this tin's untouched.

WIZARD:

Shape-Shifter requires not food.

MAN:

Fuck's sake. I'll clear this up.

MAN goes to clear up cat poo with some torn up paper. WIZARD leaps forward.

WIZARD:

But not with that! That scripture's cursed.
No, please, don't read it—

MAN:

...woah...

WIZARD:

Your eyes have drunk the Elder's hex.
You're cursed. You *have* to go.

MAN:

"We cannot give you a decision on the new claim for Disability Living Allowance yet. This is because we have requested a report from your Consultant..."

WIZARD turns away. MAN puts down paper, picks up another.

"Yesterday we sent form IS10 to you to complete. Will you please send in a copy of your tenancy agreement..."

WIZARD:

OK. Enough.

MAN:

"You should read this letter very carefully to make sure it is correct. If you think there is anything wrong, you must tell us immediately in writing."

Mate, you can't rip these up.
Don't worry. Look, I know
the things to say, their number's here,
I'll ring them back, I'll—

MAN gets out his mobile.

WIZARD:

No!

MAN:

But I don't mind. If—

WIZARD:

No!

MAN:

But why? I'll make them... understand. It's just a call—

WIZARD:

No Satan-tongue gets spoken in *my* land.

*WIZARD snatches MAN's mobile out of his hand and throws
it out the window.*

MAN:

Fuck! My phone.

WIZARD:

This is my land and you should know me better.

MAN:

OK. No calls. I'll get my phone
and then we'll write a letter.

WIZARD:

Stop trying to rhyme! Your rhymes but herald your own epic
failure! Ursula can rhyme, the carpet goblins can rhyme, but
you – can't – rhyme.

MAN:

OK, then let's be serious for a minute. If you don't reply to their—

WIZARD:

Oh, dragon's fires flame your infernal—

MAN:

No. Mate. No dragons right now. This is real. These forms
they've sent you—

WIZARD:

Don't fucking patronise me.

MAN:

What? Mate, I'm not—

WIZARD:

What the fuck do you know about being real? Tell me. The only time you feel real is here with me. You spend most of your life in a job you hate with people you hate doing something that doesn't matter to anyone. Does that make you feel 'real'? There is nothing for me in that world. But I've got a world here I love. If time were money, there'd be no one richer than me. Do you feel rich, with your 'forms' and 'meetings'? You want to come into my world as and when you like - well, that's fine. You want to manipulate me, make out your cat's got 'magic powers' just to blackmail me into pet-sitting for you - sure, that's fine, too. But don't tell me when it is and isn't 'time for dragons'. And don't tell me I need to do anything with my reality... because I've never bullied you about yours. Sort your own life out before telling me how I should change mine.

MAN:

Mate, I—

WIZARD:

Just take your shape-shif... Just take your... cat... and go. I'll see you later.

MAN:

Look, I—

WIZARD:

Yeah, I'll see you later.

Pause.

MAN:

Sure. See you later.

MAN picks up cat basket and exits.

WIZARD kneels down by kettle, slowly picks it up and then returns to chair.

There is a knock at the door.

Pause.

Another knock.

WIZARD:

Not now.

A STRANGER [V/O]:

Mr Clark? It's just me again. I came to see you yesterday? It's OK, there's no need to come to the door. I'll just pop this note under for you. I've made a few calls and I've got it all sorted for tomorrow. I know the guy you'll be seeing. He's really nice. I know public transport makes you anxious so I've arranged for a car to pick you up at 10:30. It's all in the note. Have a read when you're ready. Take care, Mr Clark.

WIZARD stands, takes a deep breath... and then smiles.

From behind the chair WIZARD fetches a small bowl, jar of pills and bottle of bleach. He keeps adding things to the bowl and grinding them up with his wooden spoon.

WIZARD:

Stride home.
Braver lone. Braver than these flats,
these haunts held back by phantom facts.

URSULA THE KETTLE [V/O]:

This is a pact one can't retract.

WIZARD:

I'll be all this place lacked...
Fantastic, like the Goddess fire,
amazed and blazed and lifted higher.

DAISUKE THE DISH RACK [V/O]:

Perspire as her flames inspire

WIZARD:

and let this dead skin tire.

URSULA THE KETTLE [V/O]:

She has a warm touch.

DAISUKE THE DISH RACK [V/O]:

Healing hand.

URSULA THE KETTLE [V/O]:

Hold tight.

DAISUKE THE DISH RACK [V/O]:

Understand.

WIZARD:

All transcans as Goddess planned.

DAISUKE THE DISH RACK [V/O]:

Heroic.

URSULA THE KETTLE [V/O]:

Brilliant.

WIZARD:

Grand.

WIZARD, URSULA [V/O] & DAISUKE [V/O]:

And I will keep strong. Walk on.
Eyes wrapped round the road home.
Keep going. Never drop.

WIZARD:

Keep wing-clipped feet from slowing.

Keep strong.
Walk on.
Watch toes
point home.
When your lonely
hopes start burning,
cover your neck,
embrace the homing.

DAISUKE THE DISH RACK [V/O]:

The homing.

URSULA THE KETTLE [V/O]:

The homing.

WIZARD:

The homing.

WIZARD lifts the bowl to his mouth and drinks.

Black out.

SCENE TEN
THE FIFTH DAY

Lights slowly up in slightly dim state on WIZARD in his chair.

MAN enters but hesitates in the flat's hall. He's wearing jeans / T-shirt.

MAN:

Hello? Um, door's open, but, um, I didn't want to just, y'know... Look, I'm sorry. I don't want us to fall out. You're right. I do hate my job. And I hate every person there. I made it two days without a poetry-spouting kettle by the skin of my teeth. I thought about bringing tinsel in for ours at work, but... well...

MAN makes his way into WIZARD's living room.

How about I get Ursula brewing and make us both a—

MAN sees WIZARD's body.

MAN touches WIZARD's hand. It is cold. MAN reels back. He gets his mobile phone, dials a number.

Black out.

SCENE ELEVEN
'STRANGERS TALK'

In darkness there is the sound of a regular phone ringing. It keeps ringing.

Ringing stops and full lights up on MAN sitting in WIZARD's flat. MAN lifts up the kettle.

MAN:

Oh, Ursula, Ursula, Ursula, spherical Ursula.

Pause.

Good morrow, noble Ursula.

Pause. MAN puts kettle down, not sure how he was expecting it to respond. MAN pulls out poem from pocket and faces the kettle.

Wish I hadn't gone,
hadn't seen Earth so hungry, slobbering soil.
Earth opened up,
dry gums parted, lipless mouth crumbling
as men I'd never met before
fed it the left-overs of your body.

Felt drunk on absence,
a hollowing spirit numbing my tongue,
double shot words dead.
Don't believe in them anyway.
Words.
My words were only ever the ghosts
of someone else's thoughts.

I stood silent. Earth devoured your scraps.

Dead words hung,
sheets of guilt, haunting,
clung round bit lips.
Still can't untie them.
They hold closed a body so full of nothing
opening up could shatter whole galaxies
under its empty weight.
My heart has sucked space inside out.
I've got the vacuum of the universe in my gut.

Kept hearing your name.
People saying your name.
No-one there knew the power
of names.

Wanted to kick ground,
yell in Earth's face,
punch out these fists so tightly squeezed
in black jacket pocket.

But didn't.
Did nothing.
Listened to strangers talk like that was you down there
falling apart in Earth's full belly.

Pause. MAN scrunches poem back into pocket.

URSULA THE KETTLE [V/O]:

He... would have liked that poem, sir.

MAN:

Ursula?

URSULA THE KETTLE [V/O]:

Yes, sir. He would've really liked it.

MAN:

No. He wouldn't have. He... he hated me writing poems.

URSULA THE KETTLE [V/O]:

He would have liked that one, sir.

DAISUKE THE DISH RACK [V/O]:

Man... levels up.

MAN:

Daisuke!

DAISUKE THE DISH RACK [V/O]:

Man earns 32 experience points.

MAN:

Yeah. Yeah, I s'pose so.

MAN turns to audience.

SCENE TWELVE
'TEA'

MAN is now at a poetry open mic night and looks out nervously across the room full of people for whom he is about to perform.

MAN:

This last poem isn't by me. It's by Wizard. He wouldn't have called himself a poet, but he was the most poetic, fantastic person I've ever known. This is called 'Tea'.

Brew for me a cuppa tea
and fill to brim my mug.
Warm our bodies, brains and speech -
internal, liquid hug.

URSULA THE KETTLE [V/O]:

Every word I form began
an undug thought to free

DAISUKE THE DISH RACK [V/O]:

each like an acorn in my skull,
to feed and wet with tea.

MAN:

You and me, together, drinking tea,
the world goes mute.
I hear a rumbling in my head,
our tea wet words take root

MAN, URSULA [V/O] & DAISUKE [V/O]:

and grow, a thousand words tower tall,
all branching inspiration.

MAN:

Kettle's boiled. Tend our talk
with tea's sweet irrigation.

Sheltered by these evergreen boughs,
make another brew.
My mind is a forest of chat
with cups of tea and you.